To my Brave Little Man

and his superhero Mom.

Published in association with Bear With Us Productions.

© 2024 My Mom Does Work!
Dan Turk

The right of Dan Turk as the author of this work has been asserted by him in accordance with the Copyright Designs and Patents Act 1988.
All rights reserved, including the right of reproduction in whole or part in any form.

ISBN Paperback: 979-8-32-005056-0
ISBN Hardback: 979-8-3302-0488-5

www.justbearwithus.com

MY MOM DOES WORK!

WRITTEN BY
DAN TURK

ILLUSTRATED BY
YEVHENIIA LISOVA

In a warm, sunny school where giggles gleam,
Went a student named **Gabriel**, to learn, play, and dream.
Each day brought a question, a teasing, a jest,
From his classmates who thought their Moms' jobs were the best.

"**Your Mom doesn't work**," they would laugh and proclaim.
"She doesn't wear suits or chase social media fame.
She doesn't go to an office, a building so tall,
So what does she even do, Gabriel? Please, tell us all!"

Gabriel sat there, **sad** and **distraught**,
Unsure how to retort, lost in his thoughts.
He knew his **Mom worked**, as busy as could be,
But whether she was

a doctor,
teacher,
or artist,

he couldn't see.

With bravery in his heart, he embarked on a quest,
To uncover the truth and put the rumors to rest.
He looked at his Mom, who worked day and night,
A whirlwind of tasks, in both darkness and light.

"**Mom, what do you do?**" he inquired with fear,
As his Mom wiped a tear from his cheek – "Oh dear!"
"Come, Gabriel," she whispered, "let's explore together,
My job is unique, and it couldn't be better."

They walked together through their cozy abode,
From room to room, with excitement that flowed.
In each new place, Gabriel's mother made clear,
What she did to keep order and everything in gear.

"Here in the kitchen, I'm a **culinary queen**,
Cooking up feasts, for each on our team.
I balance flavors, create dishes divine;
A master chef I'm not, but I do just fine."

"I make sure you're healthy, well-fed, and strong;
My job is to nurture you, all day long.
Every day is different, with needs unique,
Seven days of business, that's my workweek!"

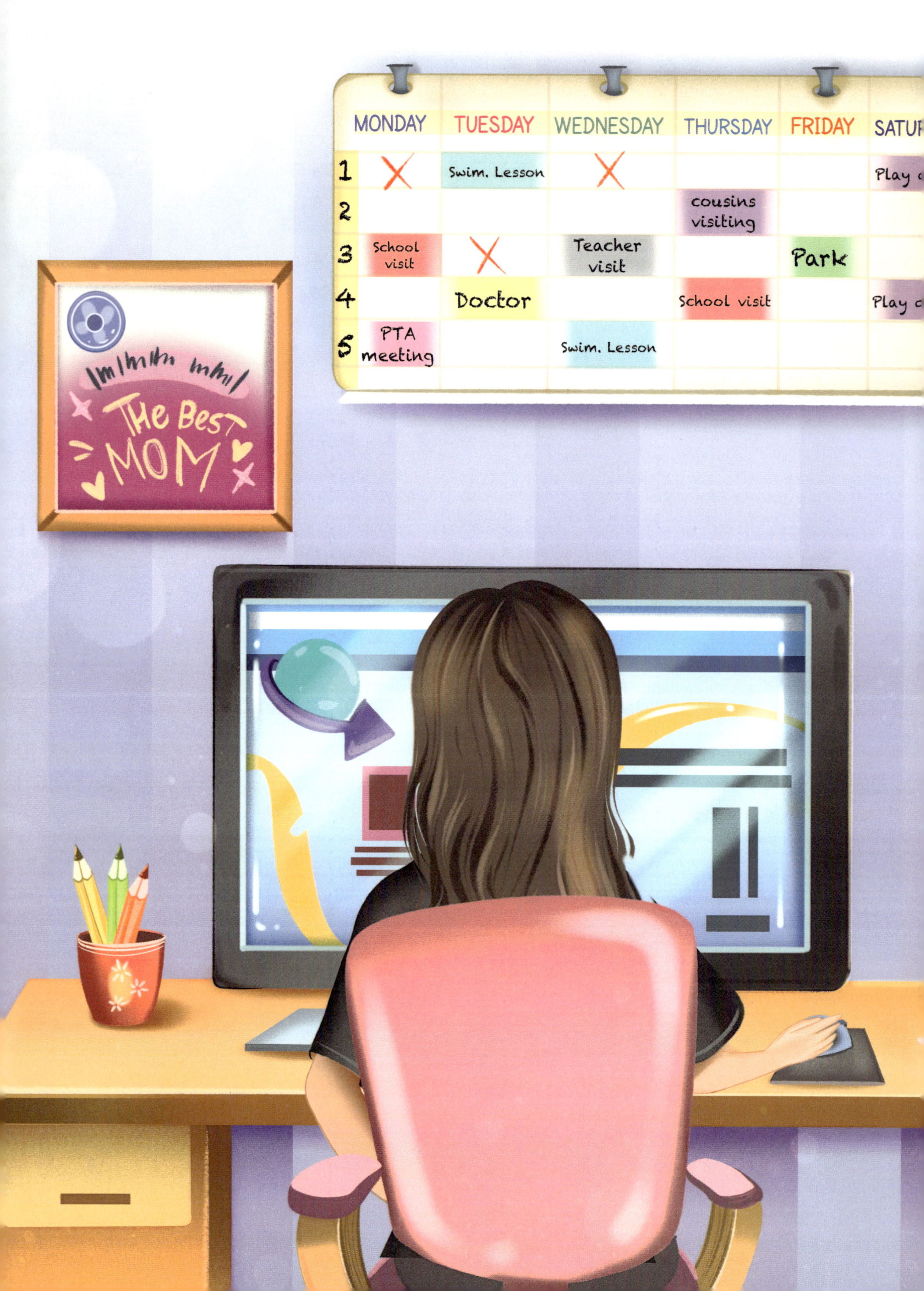
MONDAY
TUESDAY
WEDNESDAY
THURSDAY
FRIDAY
1
2
3
4
5
Swim. Lesson
cousins visiting
School visit
Teacher visit
Park
Doctor
School visit
PTA meeting
Swim. Lesson
The Best MOM

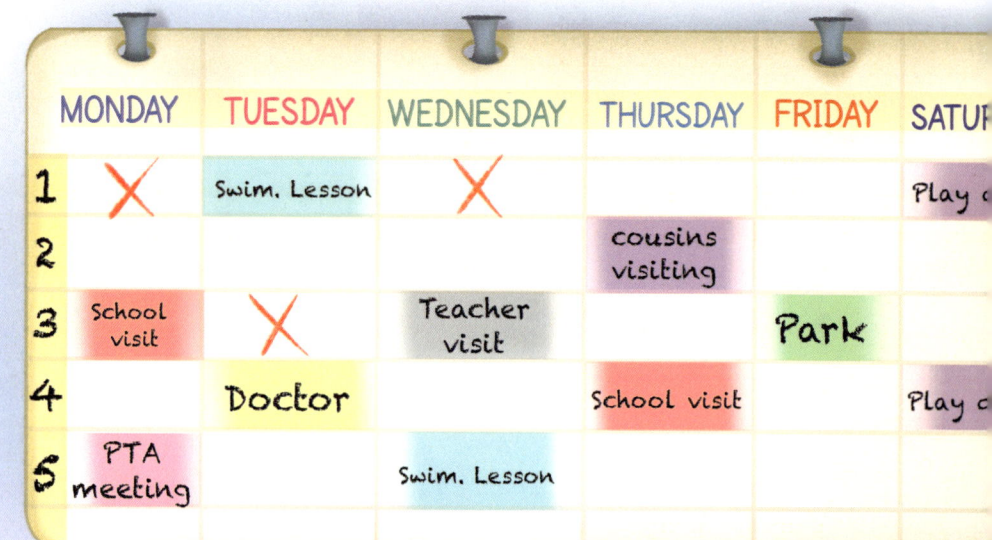

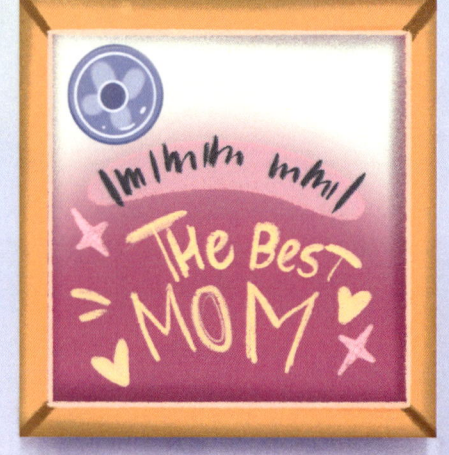

To the office they went, where bills lay in stacks:
"Here, **I'm an accountant**, our spending I track.
I schedule appointments and manage our time,
A wizard of calendars, each hour, each line."

Next, they tiptoed upstairs to a room filled with care,
A place of soft blankets, and toys everywhere.
"In this room," she explained, "**I help you** dream big and play,
Spark your imagination, to brighten your day."

"I read you stories and play make-believe,
To help you grow and learn, and freely conceive,
All that you desire, in work and life's quest;
My job is to guide you, to be your very best."

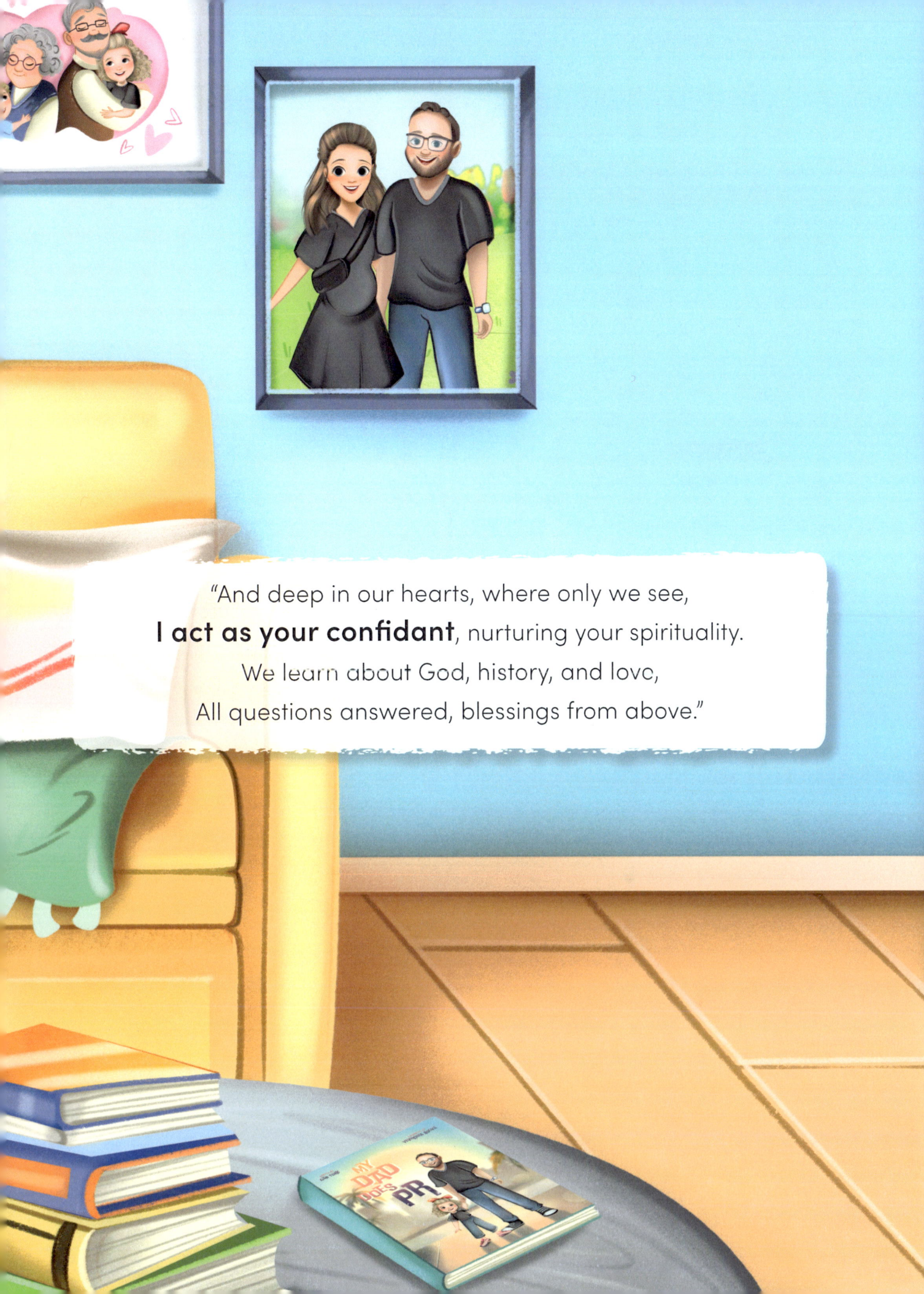

"And deep in our hearts, where only we see,
I act as your confidant, nurturing your spirituality.
We learn about God, history, and love,
All questions answered, blessings from above."

On the last stop, they ventured out to the garden so wide,
Where flowers and trees stood with grace, side by side.
"Out here, **I'm a gardener**," his Mom said with glee,
"I nurture these blossoms, set their spirits free."

"**I teach you** to cherish the beauty of Mother Earth,
To value her treasures, for all they are worth.
My job is to tend to the land and its art,
With love and with passion, right from the start."

Gabriel's eyes **sparkled**, as he started to see,
The depth of his Mom's work and creativity.
She wore many hats, each role full of heart,
A symphony of **love**, in every single part.

Armed with newfound knowledge, back to school he returned,
With **pride** and **conviction**, he eagerly churned.
The truth about his Mom, he shared with a grin,
"**She cooks, teaches, and gardens for all of our kin**."

"**She's our artist, accountant, and spiritual guide**,
Her care and attention, always fully applied.
She **nurtures** and **helps**, with love shining bright,
In everything she does, she spreads joy and light."

"**My Mom's job is real**, the most **precious** of all,
In her love and her care, I'll never fall!
All of our parents are heroes, you see,
No one more important, don't you agree?"

His classmates fell silent, their teasing put to rest,
As they heard Gabriel speak, his voice at its best:
"A job isn't measured by walls or by gold,
But the **love** and the **care** that we each choose to hold."

www.ingramcontent.com/pod-product-compliance
Lightning Source LLC
LaVergne TN
LVRC09135306O526
838201LV00019B/291